2/04

$10.95

At Home with Science

Feather and Fur!

What makes cats purr?

Written by Janice Lobb
Illustrated by Peter Utton and Ann Savage

KINGFISHER

NEW YORK

KINGFISHER
Larousse Kingfisher Chambers Inc.
95 Madison Avenue
New York, New York 10016
www.lkcpub.com

First published in 2001
10 9 8 7 6 5 4 3 2 1

1TR/1200/FR/SC/128JDA

Created and designed by Snapdragon Publishing Limited
Copyright © Snapdragon Publishing Ltd 2001

LIBRARY OF CONGRESS CATALOGING-IN-PUBLICATION DATA
has been applied for.

ISBN 0-7534-5335-5

Printed in Hong Kong

For Snapdragon
Editorial Director Jackie Fortey
Art Director Chris Legee
Designers Chris Legee and Joy Fitzsimons

For Kingfisher
Series Editor Emma Wild
Series Art Editor Mike Davis
DTP Coordinator Nicky Studdart
Production Controller Debbie Otter

Contents

About this book

Have you ever wondered how a parakeet keeps its feathers clean, or why a hamster is soft and furry while a snake is covered with scales? This book shows you all kinds of exciting things you can learn about animals with the help of family or classroom pets. You don't even need to have a pet of your own to join in the fun.

Hall of Fame

Archie and his friends are here to help you. They are each named after famous scientists—apart from Bob the (rubber) Duck, who is just a young scientist like you!

Archie
ARCHIMEDES (287–212 B.C.) The Greek scientist Archimedes figured out why things float or sink while he was in the bathtub. According to the story, he was so pleased that he leaped up, shouting "Eureka!" which means "I've done it!"

Frank
BENJAMIN FRANKLIN (1706–1790) Besides being one of the most important figures in American history, he was also a noted scientist. In a dangerous experiment in which he flew a kite in a storm, he proved that lightning is actually electricity.

Marie
MARIE CURIE (1867–1934) Girls did not go to college in Poland where Marie Curie grew up, so she went to Paris to study. Later, she worked on radioactivity and received two Nobel prizes for her discoveries, in 1903 and 1911.

Dot
DOROTHY HODGKIN (1910–1994) Dorothy Hodgkin was a British scientist who made many important discoveries about molecules and atoms, the tiny particles that make up everything around us. She was given the Nobel prize for Chemistry in 1964.

See for yourself!

1 Read the science facts about animals, then try the "See for yourself!" experiments to see them in action. In science, experiments are used to find or show the answers.

2 Carefully read the instructions for each experiment, making sure you follow the numbered steps in the correct order.

3 Here are some of the things you will need. Have everything ready before you start each experiment.

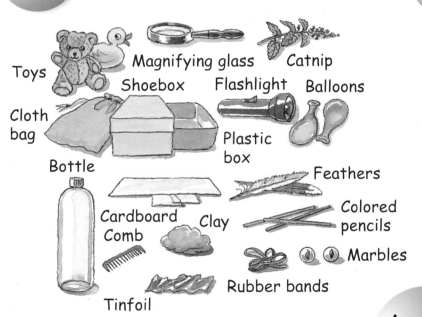

Toys
Magnifying glass
Catnip
Shoebox
Flashlight
Balloons
Cloth bag
Plastic box
Bottle
Feathers
Cardboard
Clay
Colored pencils
Comb
Marbles
Rubber bands
Tinfoil

4 ## Safety first! ✋

All the experiments are safe. Just make sure that you tell an adult what you are doing and get their help when you see the warning sign. Remember to always wash your hands after you have handled your pet.

Amazing facts

WOW!

You'll notice that some words are written in *italics*. You can learn more about them in the glossary at the end of the book. And if you want to find out some amazing facts, keep an eye out for the "Wow!" panels.

Keep an eye out for useful tips!

Have fun!

How does my cat purr?

Why can cats do no wrong?

Because they are purr-fect!

Sound is a kind of *energy* that is carried to our ears by movements in the air. When a cat purrs, it puts sound energy into the air by moving part of its throat back and forth quickly. This motion is called a *vibration*. Every sound you hear is made by something vibrating. It could be a surface, a string, or air blown through a musical instrument. It is difficult to see air moving because it is invisible, but you can see surfaces and strings vibrate, and you can hear them make the air move.

Making sounds

A cat purrs at the back of its throat, but when it meows, it uses its *vocal cords*. Air pushed out from the lungs makes the vocal cords vibrate.

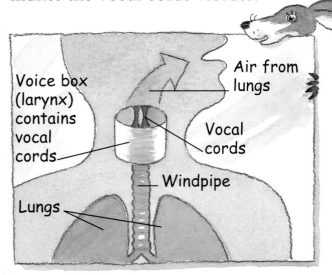

Voice box (larynx) contains vocal cords

Air from lungs

Vocal cords

Windpipe

Lungs

A cat has a high voice.

A lion has a deep voice.

High notes vibrate in your head— low ones in your chest.

Small animals have higher voices because they have short vocal cords. Big animals have longer vocal cords and deeper voices.

Human voices sound different when they sing. Air vibrates in the throat, mouth, chest, and face, too. Try it!

6

See for yourself! 🖐

1 All you need to make a drum is a hollow container and a stretchy "drum skin," such as a popped rubber balloon, to attach over the open end. Try different sizes for different sounds.

Jar

Plastic container

Bottle

2 Make a model guitar from a shoebox or an ice-cream container. Ask a grown-up to cut a notch in each side.

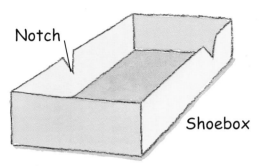

Notch

Shoebox

3 Slide a ruler into the notches, so that it slants across the box. Put rubber bands around the box, so they rest on the edge of the ruler.

Ruler

Rubber bands

4 Now twang the rubber bands. You can see them vibrate. You can hear that long ones make a low sound, and short ones make a high sound.

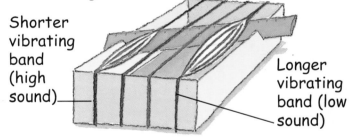

Shorter vibrating band (high sound)

Longer vibrating band (low sound)

WOW! Silence in space!

There is no sound in outer space, because there is no air to carry vibrations. In space, no one can even hear you shout!

The sound of a dog barking can annoy some people!

7

Why does my goldfish look sad?

Because it's feeling gill-ty!

How do fish swim?

When most fish swim, they swing their tail fins from side to side and curve their bodies to the left and right, pushing against the water. The water pushes back, and the fish move forward. Most fish are heavier than water, so they have no difficulty sinking down. To help them float back up, however, many fish have a bag of air called a *swim bladder*. They fill this with gases taken from their blood, which makes them buoyant, or able to float. Fish are able to float at any depth without effort.

Streamlined shapes

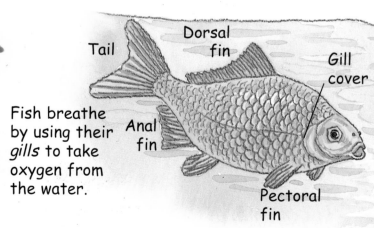

Flying fish

Tail

Dorsal fin

Gill cover

Swim bladder

Fish breathe by using their *gills* to take oxygen from the water.

Anal fin

Pectoral fin

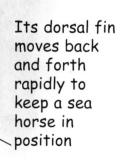

Its dorsal fin moves back and forth rapidly to keep a sea horse in position

To move forward, a fish moves its body from side to side. Its fins help keep it upright, and they also steer it in the right direction.

Fish that swim fast have a smooth, streamlined shape. Some fish, such as flying fish, can swim so fast they are able to leap right out of the water.

Fish with shapes that are awkward, like the sea horse, are extremely weak swimmers.

8

See for yourself!

1 To make a diving model, take half a plastic drinking straw. Seal the top with a small piece of modeling clay, then seal the bottom with a big piece of clay.

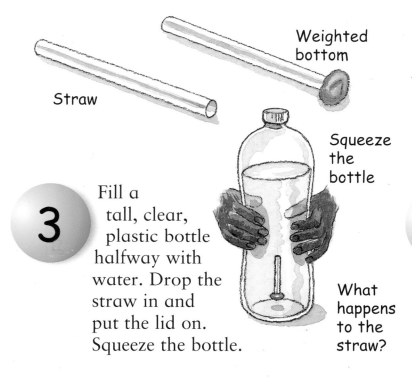

Straw

Weighted bottom

2 Test the straw in a bowl of water. It should float upright below the surface. If it bobs up out of the water, add more clay to make it sink. If it touches the bottom, take a little off.

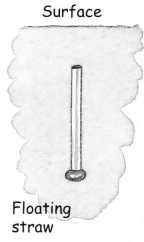

Surface

Floating straw

3 Fill a tall, clear, plastic bottle halfway with water. Drop the straw in and put the lid on. Squeeze the bottle.

Squeeze the bottle

What happens to the straw?

4 When you squeeze the sides of the bottle, your straw sinks, like a fish diving. When you let go, the straw floats back up again.

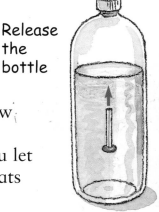

Release the bottle

Sharks on the move

WOW!

Sharks differ from other fish because they must swim constantly. Sharks cannot pump water over their gills for oxygen. Swimming forces water through their mouths and over their gills, allowing oxygen to go to their blood. Most sharks do not have a swim bladder, so swimming also helps keep them from sinking.

Water in through the mouth

Water out through the gills

Water plants help to make oxygen for fish.

9

Can pets talk to us?

How does your pet tell you that it wants to be fed? Does it make a noise or let you know in some other way? Animals do not have conversations, but they can give each other, and us, very clear messages. The sounds they make and their silent signals are called body language. They show us what a pet is thinking or feeling. If we know what to look for, we can tell whether animals are well and happy or are feeling sad and unwell.

What does a cat say if you step on its tail?

Me-OW!

Sending signals

A sad dog

A dog with its tail between its legs is miserable, while a happy dog wags its tail. A cat swishes its tail to show that it is angry and holds its tail upright when it is content.

Not all signals are understood by humans. Some animals use *ultrasonic* sounds to communicate. Some animals leave scent messages to tell other animals "I was here."

An angry cat

A dog sniffing scent messages

A parrot does not make sounds the same way we do.

Polly wanna cracker!

A "talking" bird mimics sounds that it has heard. It doesn't actually understand what it is saying.

See for yourself!

1 Watch a dog when it is very pleased to see someone. It wags its tail and rolls over on its back to have its tummy rubbed.

2 When a cat is pleased to see you, it rubs itself against your legs and purrs loudly. It wants you to pet it.

3 But watch it when it is scared by a dog. It arches its back, fluffs out its fur, and tries to look big and fierce.

4 Listen to the sounds pigeons and doves make. They communicate by cooing to each other, and they even coo to their eggs.

Long-distance call!

WOW!

Animals like to guard their territory and keep intruders away. Lions can roar loudly to warn rival lions to stay away. They can be heard from as far as five miles away.

Learn to understand your pet.

What can my dog hear?

What music does your dog like to listen to?

Rock and roll over!

A dog has very good hearing. Sound traveling through the air is collected by the ear flaps on a dog's head and sent to the eardrums inside. Eardrums are round patches of skin that vibrate when sound reaches them. These sound vibrations then reach the *inner ear,* which sends messages to the *brain.* If you look at a frog or a lizard, you can see what eardrums look like—they are on the outside of their heads.

Sound sensations

A dog's eardrum, like yours, is hidden inside its head. Behind the eardrum is the inner ear. In the inner ear is a spiral-shaped organ called the cochlea. It can pick up high, medium, and low sounds.

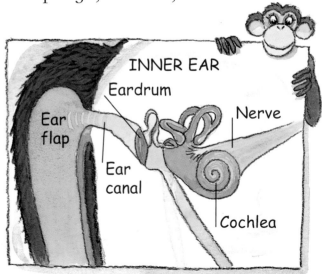

INNER EAR

Eardrum

Nerve

Ear flap

Ear canal

Cochlea

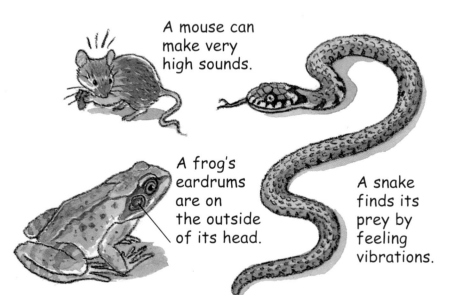

A mouse can make very high sounds.

A frog's eardrums are on the outside of its head.

A snake finds its prey by feeling vibrations.

Many small animals, such as mice and bats, can hear ultrasonic sounds, which humans cannot hear. Dogs can hear these high pitches, too.

Snakes and fish are deaf, but their bodies can feel even the slightest vibrations coming through the ground or water.

See for yourself!

1 Imagine what it would be like to be a snake—if you could feel vibrations coming through the air. Put your hands on a speaker when music is playing. Can you feel the beat?

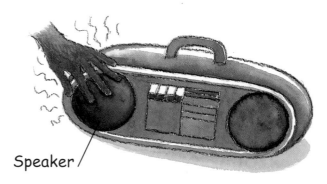

Speaker

2 Wrap some thin paper around a comb. It makes a simple musical instrument.

Comb

3 Pout your lips, and put the comb against them. Now make a tooting noise, so that the paper vibrates. Try to toot a tune. The vibrations will tickle your lips.

WOW! Bouncing sound!

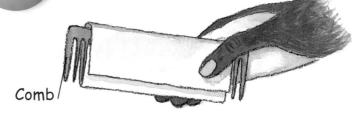

When flying, bats use *echolocation* to catch moths. Dolphins in the sea also use echolocation to find schools of fish. These animals bounce sounds off objects and wait for the echoes to come back. This tells them how far away their next meal is, and how fast they have to go to catch it.

Do not upset fish or reptiles by tapping on their tanks.

Do not disturb!

Why is my hamster soft?

Like most *mammals*, hamsters are covered in hair. Their hair feels soft—it is fine and short and bends easily when you touch it. Touching an animal with longer, coarser hair, such as a shaggy dog, feels different. Chicks are covered in fine, soft feathers called down. Soft, fluffy animals are usually *warm-blooded*. Their hair or feathers trap air next to their bodies, acting as *insulation* and keeping them warm.

> Where did the hamster go on vacation?

> Hamster-dam!

Cold-blooded creatures

Earthworms are *cold-blooded*. They don't have a furry covering because they breathe through their skin.

A worm has no fluff to keep it warm.

Birds have feathers, which are like branched hairs.

Turtles have shells and scaly skin.

Reptiles are not fluffy because they are also cold-blooded creatures. They need the sun to shine on their scaly skin to warm themselves up.

Some insects look fluffy, although they are not warm-blooded. Be careful! They are not as cuddly as they look.

Bees may sting.

Some caterpillars are poisonous. Do not touch!

See for yourself!

1 Does everything that looks soft feel the same? Pick two toys that look fluffy and two toys that look smooth.

Felt teddy bear

Rubber ball

Wood train

Cotton block

Wood mouse

Plastic duck

2 Ask someone to put one of the toys in a bag. Put your hand in the bag and see if your fingers can tell whether it is a smooth or fluffy toy. Can you also feel what it is from its shape and size?

Bag

3 Compare the fluffy toys and the smooth toys. Which ones feel warmer to the touch? Do any of them feel cold?

Prickly Hair

WOW!

Quill

A porcupine is covered with coarse hair and sharp quills.

A porcupine has long, soft hairs and strong, stiff quills on its back, sides, and tail. The long, sharp quills are actually long hairs that are stuck together. Quills protect the porcupine from its enemies.

Don't pet animals without their owner's permission.

15

How does my rabbit hop?

What happens if you make a rabbit angry?

It gets hopping mad!

If you watch a rabbit, you will see that it moves differently from a cat or dog—it hops. This is because its back legs are longer than its front legs. Strong leg muscles push its hind feet back against the ground, and this *force* shoots its body forward. Its front feet go to the ground to balance it as it lands. Its speed and hopping height protect a rabbit from its enemies.

What can hop?

Most frogs have strong legs for hopping and for swimming, too.

Frog

The kangaroo's tail helps it balance as it leaps along.

Rabbit

Dot

Archie

A rabbit's legs store energy for the next hop.

Kangaroos have long, strong hind legs, so they can hop without using their small front legs. They balance themselves with their tails.

An elephant's front and back legs are the same length, so it cannot hop. When an elephant walks, it lifts only one foot off the ground at a time.

See for yourself!

1 Watch animals move, and try copying them. It is hard because our bodies are shaped differently from most animals'. Try being a snake and wriggle on the floor without using your arms and legs.

Marie being a snake

2 Try lifting yourself off the floor like a lizard or a crocodile, with your arms and legs bent and sticking out to the side. It is very tiring for your muscles.

Marie being a crocodile

3 Straighten your arms and legs underneath you, like a horse or elephant. Your arms are too short, so you may fall on your face!

Marie being a horse

4 It is easier if you bend your legs, let your arms hang down, and walk like a chimpanzee. Or you can bend your legs and hop like a frog or a rabbit.

Marie being a frog

WOW!

High jumps!

A flea can jump a hundred times its own body height. It stores energy in special pads where its legs join its body. This stored energy is released as the flea jumps, giving extra power to push it through the air.

Can you play hopscotch?

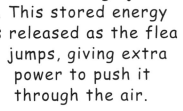

Can my cat see in the dark?

A cat can see well both in daylight and at night, but no animal can see if it is totally dark. An animal needs light to reach the *retina* at the back of its eyes to be able to see. The retina sends a message to the brain, which figures out what the eye has seen. *Nocturnal* animals come out at night, and they have special eyes that make the most of what light there is. They also use other senses, like hearing, to find their way.

Which cats don't go out late at night?

Scaredy-cats!

Night sight

Like people, cats have *pupils,* which control the amount of light that enters the eye. In bright light, the pupils are small; in dim light, they widen.

Unlike people, cats have a mirrorlike lens in the back of each eye. It helps them see in dim light, and it causes eye shine, the glow of a cat's eyes at night.

Some nocturnal animals, such as a bush baby, have very big eyes to help them see in dim light.

Pupil

Pupil

Daytime   Nighttime

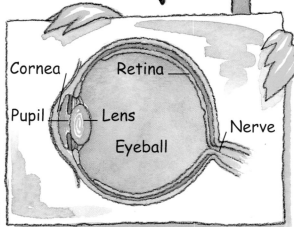

Cornea   Retina

Pupil   Lens

Eyeball   Nerve

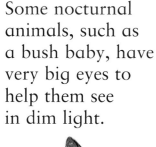

Bush baby

See for yourself!

1 Glass marbles are the same shape as eyeballs but, unlike eyes, they let in light from all sides.

Flashlight

Marbles

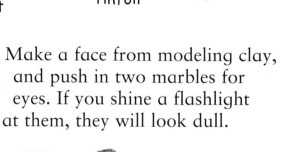
Modeling clay

Tinfoil

2 Make a face from modeling clay, and push in two marbles for eyes. If you shine a flashlight at them, they will look dull.

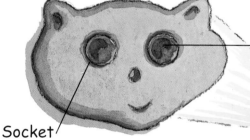
Marble

Socket

Flashlight

3 Now line the eye sockets with shiny tinfoil before you push the eyes in. They will shine like cats' eyes when you turn your flashlight on them.

Tinfoil

Flashlight

Snake

WOW!

Hot on the trail!

At night some snakes hunt small rodents. Little heat-sensitive *pit organs* near their nostrils pick up the body heat of their warm-blooded prey. They do not need to see the prey with their eyes.

Mouse

Be careful in the dark—don't trip over things!

How does my bird keep clean?

What do you give a dirty bird?

Beauty tweetment!

Animals need to keep their skin, fur, or feathers in good condition to prevent disease. Many spend a lot of time cleaning themselves to remove little creatures, called *parasites*, that live on their bodies. Some pets need help from their owners to brush out long, tangled fur. Birds, however, clean their feathers with their beaks—a process called *preening*. Some birds bathe while swimming, others wet their feathers in puddles or birdbaths. If no water is available, many birds will take a dust bath.

See for yourself!

1 Collect some of the feathers that fall out of your bird's cage, or look at feathers in clothes or decorations.

Vane (flat area)

Barbs (hook together to make the vane)

Thick shaft down the middle

Contour feather

2 Contour feathers are smooth and give the bird a streamlined surface. Downy feathers, which keep the bird warm, have a thinner shaft and are fluffy.

Thin shaft

Fluffy branches

Downy feather

Good grooming

A bird has a long neck so that it can reach the preen gland under its tail. It spreads oil from this gland onto its feathers to make them *waterproof*.

Cats and dogs use their front incisor teeth to comb their fur and remove the dirt and tangles. A dog nibbles its fur with its teeth and licks it clean with its wet tongue.

Birds use their beaks to press together and refasten the hooks of the barbs in their feathers to keep them strong.

A cat uses its rough tongue to wash itself. The tongue's surface is covered with tiny hooks that groom the fur— working like a brush and comb.

Flying pens

WOW!

Large wing feathers from geese were once used to make quill pens. The end of the hollow shaft was sliced off and shaped into a pointed tip, which was then dipped in ink for writing.

Always be gentle with your pet!

21

Why does my snake have scales?

Why do snakes make bad musicians?

Because they don't practice their scales!

Have you ever wondered why a snake's skin is covered with *scales*? Like other animals, a snake's body is made up mostly of water and would soon dry out in the air if it didn't have a waterproof layer on the outside. Water is lost from the surface of an animal's body by *evaporation*. If an animal loses too much water, it will die. The waterproof scales that cover a snake's body help keep water in and stop it from drying out. They also protect the snake as it slithers over rough ground.

Skin types

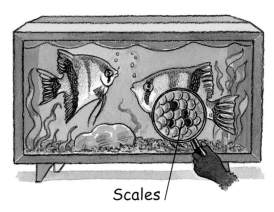

Scales

Scales protect the skin of fish from drying out in salty seawater. They also prevent fish from getting waterlogged in fresh water.

Mammals, such as mice, have an outer layer of oily skin under their fur to keep them waterproof.

Mice

Animals that do not have waterproof skin must live in damp places. For example, earthworms and frogs have soft, moist skin that dries out quickly in the air.

Frog

Earthworms

See for yourself!

1 Draw the outline of a fish or a snake on a piece of cardboard.

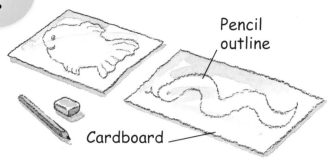

Pencil outline

Cardboard

2 Cut out scales from colored pieces of paper, or use some colored stickers.

3 Starting at the tail end, stick on overlapping scales to cover the shape you have drawn.

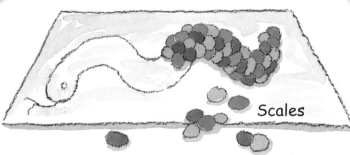

Scales

4 If you use pieces of modeling clay, you can make your animal armor-plated.

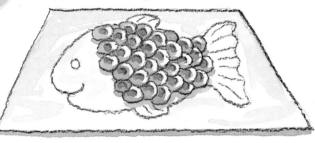

Modeling clay

WOW! **Armor-plated!**

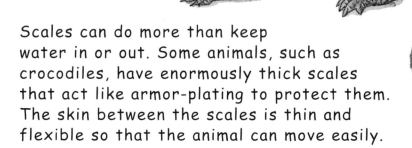

Scales can do more than keep water in or out. Some animals, such as crocodiles, have enormously thick scales that act like armor-plating to protect them. The skin between the scales is thin and flexible so that the animal can move easily.

Never touch an animal in the wild!

Why is my mouse brown?

The color of an animal's fur or feathers helps protect it. Sunlight can be harmful because it contains *ultraviolet light,* which can cause a sunburn. An animal's color is like sunblock, preventing its skin from burning. The color of skin, hair, fur, and feathers comes from *melanin,* which is produced by an animal's body. Black or brown animals produce a lot of melanin and are more protected in the sun than light-colored animals. An animal's color also helps it blend into its habitat, allowing it to hide. This is called *camouflage.*

Eeeek!

When is it bad luck to see a black cat?

When you're a mouse!

Eye colors

The colored part of the eye is called the iris. If it is brown, it contains a lot of melanin. This protects the eye from bright sunlight.

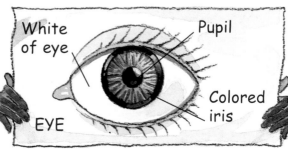

White of eye

Pupil

EYE

Colored iris

Green iris

Eyes with less melanin are blue, green, or even yellow.

People and animals with no melanin at all are called albinos. They have white hair and skin and pink irises, and they need to stay out of the sun.

See for yourself!

1 Look at your family and pets. Make drawings of their eyes. How many different colors can you see?

2 Can you find hairs and feathers that have fallen out around the house? Dark hairs are hard to see on dark furniture and clothes.

Hair

3 Paint and cut out a picture of an animal that has several colors in its fur. Paint a background in the same colors. If you cannot see the animal against the background, it is camouflaged.

Fine feathers

WOW!

Flamingo

Drake

Ducks

Birds have even more colors than mammals. Flamingos are pink because the shrimp they eat contain a pink substance called carotene. Some birds have tiny, hollow "bubbles" in their feathers that *refract,* or split up, light, creating rainbow colors. Female birds choose the males with the brightest colors.

Always protect your skin—it can easily burn.

What does my guinea pig eat?

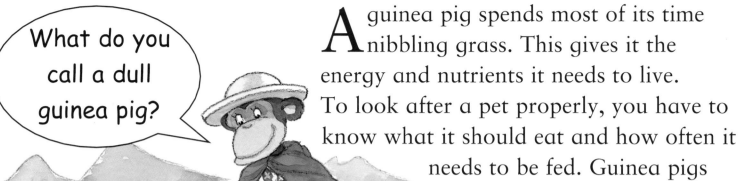

What do you call a dull guinea pig?

A herbi-bore!

A guinea pig spends most of its time nibbling grass. This gives it the energy and nutrients it needs to live. To look after a pet properly, you have to know what it should eat and how often it needs to be fed. Guinea pigs eat plants because they are *herbivores*. Their wild relatives in South America eat grass, roots, and shoots. If pet guinea pigs are kept indoors and cannot have fresh grass, they will eat hay, which is dried grass and mixtures of seed.

Pets' menu

If animals are kept as pets, they must have the right food. Guinea pigs, rabbits, and gerbils are herbivores, and so are stick insects.

Animals, like this chameleon, that need to eat a lot of live, wriggly insects are called insectivores.

In the wild, *carnivores*, like dogs and cats, eat other animals. Canned pet food has to contain the balance of nutrients a dog or cat needs.

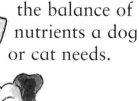

Menu
Grass
Fresh hay

Menu
Nuts & seeds

Menu
Leaves
Bushes

Menu
Crickets

Menu
Meat

See for yourself!

1 Animals know what they like. Let a guinea pig choose between a dish of cat food and a pile of hay. It will eat the hay because it is a herbivore.

Cat food   Hay

2 Do the same with a cat, and it will turn its nose up at the hay. Cats eat meat. They are carnivores.

Hay

Cat food

3 Put a dish of cat food in front of a dog. It will eat it. It is a carnivore, too—and it cannot read labels.

Cat food

4 Do mice and rats really like cheese? Try it and see, but only give them a little. Too much may make them sick.

Mouse   Rat

Chubby cheeks!

WOW!

Hamsters have special pouches in their cheeks, so if there is plenty of food, they can collect it and carry it away to store it. A tiny hamster can fit seeds as large as acorns snugly in its cheeks.

Guinea pigs need food containing vitamin C.

Why does my dog play?

Have you ever watched a puppy chase a ball or pounce on its mother's tail? In the wild, most grown-up animals don't play. They are too busy just staying alive. When baby animals play, they are practicing the skills they will need when they grow up. Young carnivores pretend to hunt and have play fights to figure out which one is boss. Animals, such as dogs, that we keep as pets often stay playful even when they are grown-up.

Why does a dog chase its tail?

To make both ends meet!

Fun and games

Watch some of the things different animals do to amuse themselves. Dogs enjoy chasing sticks and bringing them back.

A parakeet will play with its mirror.

Lambs and baby goats run around playing "king of the castle" in their pastures.

Intelligent animals, such as monkeys, need plenty of things to do. Otherwise they get bored.

See for yourself!

1 Pets do not need expensive toys. Tie a folded paper "butterfly" to a piece of string, and trail it in front of a cat. It will be happy to pounce on it.

2 Hold the butterfly up above the cat's head. It will reach up and bat it with its paws.

3 Fill up a little cloth bag with catnip, and your cat will play with it for hours.

Cloth mouse

Cloth bag

Catnip

Tie up the end

4 Wash out an empty plastic milk container for your dog. He will chase it if you throw it—and play tug-of-war.

Milk container

Play school!

WOW!

Porpoises and dolphins are the only wild animals that actually choose to play with humans. They follow boats and sometimes approach swimmers near the beach.

Pets need peace and quiet as well as play time.

Pets quiz

1 Where does a cat make purring sounds?
  a) In its throat
  b) In its tail
  c) In its tummy

2 What does a hamster's soft fur do?
  a) It helps keep it warm
  b) It helps it breathe
  c) It helps keep it dry

3 What does a bird use to clean itself?
  a) Its beak
  b) Its tongue
  c) Its teeth

4 What does a fish use to float up in water?
  a) Its gills
  b) Its scales
  c) Its swim bladder

5 When does a dog put its tail between its legs?
  a) When it is miserable
  b) When it is happy
  c) When it is angry

6 Which pair of legs is longer on a rabbit?
  a) The back legs
  b) The front legs
  c) Neither—they are the same

7 Which part of a cat's eye gets larger at night?
  a) The retina
  b) The iris
  c) The pupil

8 What is a snake's body covered with?
  a) Fur
  b) Feathers
  c) Scales

9 What is an animal with white hair and pink eyes called?
  a) A palomino
  b) An albino
  c) A pigment

10 What is the name given to an animal that eats only plants?
  a) A carnivore
  b) A herbivore
  c) An insectivore

Answers on page 32

Glossary

Brain
The organ inside the skull that receives information from the body and tells it what to do.

Camouflage
Coloring or shape that helps hide an animal in its environment.

Carnivores
Animals that catch and eat other animals or eat those killed by others.

Cold-blooded
Animals that cannot make their own body heat. They get heat from their surroundings.

Echolocation
The system used by bats and dolphins to navigate in the dark.

Energy
The ability to do work or make something happen.

Evaporation
When a liquid turns into a gas or vapor.

Force
A push or pull that can change something's movement or shape.

Gills
Delicate organs behind a fish's head used for absorbing oxygen from the water into the fish's blood.

Herbivores
Animals that eat only plant materials.

Inner ear
The internal part of the ear that is sensitive to sound vibrations and head movements.

Insulation
A material used to keep heat or cold from escaping.

Mammals
Animals that breathe air, are covered in hair, are warm-blooded, and have a bony skeleton.

Melanin
The pigment in the skin of animals, in all shades from yellow to black, that protects against ultraviolet light.

Nocturnal
Awake and active during the night.

Parasites
Small animals that live and feed on a larger animal, either inside it or on its skin.

Pit organs
A heat-sensitive organ located between the eyes and nostrils on the sides of a snake's head. It allows snakes to locate their prey from the body heat the animal gives off.

Preening
When a bird uses its beak to comb its feathers and to make them waterproof with oil from its preen gland.

Pupil
The round hole or slit in the center of the iris through which light enters the eye.

Refract
To change the direction in which light is traveling. This can make something look like it has changed size or color.

Retina
The layer at the back of the eye that sends messages to the brain when light falls on it.

Scales
Waterproof plates that form a layer over the skin of reptiles and some fish.

Swim bladder
A long, thin bag just under a fish's backbone that can be filled with air to help it float.

Ultrasonic
High-frequency sounds that are above the range of human hearing.

Ultraviolet light
Extremely strong light that cannot be seen by the human eye, but can be harmful if someone is exposed to it for a period of time.

Vibration
When an object goes back and forth rapidly.

Vocal cords
Folds of tissue over the voice box that can be tightened or relaxed to affect the noise a human or an animal makes.

Warm-blooded
Mammals and birds whose bodies are warmed by energy released from food.

Waterproof
Will not let water pass through or stick to it.

Index

Answers to the Pets quiz on page 30
1 a 2 a 3 a 4 c 5 a 6 a 7 c 8 c 9 b 10 b